living like
AUDREY

living like
AUDREY

Life Lessons *from the* Fairest Lady of All

VICTORIA LOUSTALOT

Guilford, Connecticut

Dedication

For my grandmother, because she was born just 366 days after Audrey and because, if they had ever had the chance to meet, they would have understood each other.

Contents

Funny Face, 1957

Introduction

When I took on the task of writing about Audrey Hepburn, one of the first things I did was start talking about it. Everyone, even men, had the same reaction. It didn't matter where I was, either. It happened first in a park in Brooklyn; later at a restaurant in Los Angeles; then at the front desk of a hotel in Amsterdam; and eventually inside one of those office complexes in Manhattan that are enormous but feel claustrophobic.

At the first mention of Audrey's name, somebody would get a spark in their eye and pipe up, *Oh, I love Audrey!* This would be followed by another somebody expressing their own bubbly tidbit of approval and enthusiasm, and by then all of the eyes in the group would be ablaze. I'd respond by offering a brief summary of Audrey's story, working in at some point, casually, that she wasn't an American, not by birth, not by blood, not even by residence.

This fact would inevitably lead to the second recurring reaction. People would look surprised, but only one person would say what the rest were thinking: *She wasn't?* And every time, I could practically hear the thoughts bobbling among the group: *But she was such a Hollywood star. She didn't have an accent…*

Well, she *was* an actress.

More than a few of our friends across the pond in Britain have fallen for their own version of this phenomenon. *Of course she wasn't American. She was British,* several have said to me, not once hesitating to assert what they were certain was her obvious nationality. In a technically legal, stuffy sense, they weren't exactly wrong. Still, the Belgians might beg to differ, and they have a strong case.

Because it was in Brussels that Audrey was born on May 4, 1929. Her mother was a Dutch baroness from Arnhem, and her father was a professional ne'er-do-well from the Czech Republic. It was actually Audrey's paternal grandfather, and he alone, who was born in London. According to British law, however, this generational link, even leapfrogging as it had from grandfather to granddaughter, was sufficient to make Audrey herself English. Who would have thought the British would be so lenient about, well, anything, but especially citizenship? It is also true that, before World War II, Audrey attended boarding school in England and that she did use a British passport for most of her adult travels.

So while the Belgians still have the most legitimate claim to Audrey's patrimony, the Brits may also lay claim rightly enough to a slice of her heritage. But, then, so, too, may the Dutch. For not only was Audrey's mother Dutch, but when the war did come, it was Audrey's father, already largely absent from her life, who arrived at her English boarding school and rushed her onto one of the last orange planes, on which he left the ten-year-old to fly by herself to Holland. It is hard to imagine that moment as anything other than some kind of familial version of *Casablanca*'s final, devastating scene.

It would be twenty years before Audrey saw her father again. Not that the passage of decades changed much. Their reunion was undoubtedly many things, but, by all accounts from those who were present or were told about it in intimacy and confidence not long after, it was most essentially lonely. The adjective may strike some as unexpected in this context, perhaps, but it is unlikely to have surprised Audrey herself. By that time in her life, she knew something of F. Scott Fitzgerald's meaning when he wrote, "Things are sweeter when they're lost. I know because once I wanted something and got it. It was the only thing I ever wanted, and when I got it, it turned to dust in my hand."

Audrey spent the rest of the war with her mother in and around Arnhem. They lived under the German occupation of the Netherlands, experiencing firsthand the harrowing consequences of the failed Allied maneuver "Operation Market Garden" in September 1944, as well as the Hongerwinter ("Hunger winter"), or Dutch famine, which followed at the end of 1944 and into 1945. During the last year of the war, like many families, Audrey and her mother lived mostly off of tulips, which they ground into flour to make something resembling bread.

By the time Allied troops liberated the Netherlands in May of 1945, Audrey was severely malnourished, suffering from anemia, edema, and respiratory problems. She had very nearly died during the war and understood its repercussions in ways none of her civilian peers in America could.

And yet, that has not prevented Americans from their persistence in trying to claim Audrey for their own as much as Europeans do—perhaps, unsurprisingly, even more so. It doesn't matter that she didn't set foot on United States soil until the French told her to, which is exactly what happened when the eminent writer Colette spotted Audrey on a beach in France and demanded she be cast as Gigi in the forthcoming theatrical premiere of the eponymously titled *Gigi* on Broadway.

That New York play is what led to Audrey's Hollywood screen test and her subsequent casting in *Roman Holiday*.

Never mind that the role sent her right back to Europe and to Italy, where filming took place on location throughout Rome. Never mind, because as soon as the movie opened stateside, Audrey was a genuine star. Within months Hollywood would go on to award the twenty-four-year-old starlet the best actress Oscar for her turn as the royal Princess Ann, cementing her status as Hollywood royalty.

It was an award that everyone agreed she deserved, no one more so than her leading man in the film, Gregory Peck. "She was the most extraordinary, natural actress, but not even so much an actress as a person of great, great quality, great depth, great intelligence, great humor, a wonderful, wonderful lady. I treasure in my recollections of my career those six months that we spent in Rome. Probably the happiest experience that I had making movies," Peck would tell a reporter many decades later, near the end of his life. And such praise from an esteemed actor who you might say was nothing short of the male Audrey Hepburn, for who is more gracious and more lovely than Gregory Peck? Only Audrey.

When Audrey careens across the golden screen on that little Vespa, flying through Rome, we are all Gregory Peck in that moment—a little taken aback (who is this charming, gutsy waif?) and entirely delighted (whoever she is, we know we don't want to lose sight of her for even an instant).

A very young Audrey, still physically frail from the war and struggling to make a living as a dancer and performer in London, took to Gigi and the American stage and then to Hollywood's camera like quicksilver, determined to take fast advantage of

---

66 Audrey really cared and really listened. Most people don't. If you really listen, it's because you really care. I don't listen to half of what I hear—but Audrey did. 99

—DORIS BRYNNER,
model and the wife of actor Yul Brynner

---

the new life before her. That she went on to have remarkable onscreen success and earn a flawless off-screen reputation speaks not merely to opportunities seized but to the qualities that Peck recognized in her: her extraordinary, natural acting ability and her singular depth, intelligence, and humor.

I can't forget, either, that Audrey's first starring role, which so captivated Peck and subsequently the rest of us, was as a princess, one whose country is never identified, never even hinted at, during the entirety of the film. Of course it wasn't. It would have been wholly unnecessary and even false to attempt to select a single place of origin for not only the character of Princess Ann but for the actress who played her. It is this universality of appeal along with her combination of worthy attributes that makes each of us fall in love with Audrey the first time we see her in *Roman Holiday*, and keeps each of us in love with her ever after.

One might be tempted to ask (not you or me but some uninformed poor soul out there), why live like Audrey? Isn't living like Audrey impossible, given the icon that she was? But it's not. Bringing a little more Audrey into your life is as easy as following her lead.

Connie Wald, who was one of Audrey's closest friends for much of her life, summarized Audrey's legacy perfectly when she said, "Quite a lovely heritage she's left in this world. The films people can see and the joy that she gives them. And I can think of no more beautiful model to try to be like for the young people today and not many like her that one would want to emulate."

In the movie *Sabrina*, Audrey plays Sabrina Fairchild, the daughter of a chauffeur. Late in the story, Sabrina's father says to her, with a bit of sadness for his own life and family and a bit of fear for his child's life and future, "You're still the chauffeur's daughter, and you're still reaching for the moon." And Sabrina replies, "No, father. The moon is reaching for me."

Throughout her life, Audrey let the moon reach for her, thereby showing us how to live, if we would let her. 👓

Chapter 1

THE POWER
OF BEING
UNASSUMING

"There are certain shades of limelight that can wreck a girl's complexion."

—*Audrey*

as Holly Golightly in
Breakfast at Tiffany's

Charade, 1963

Sean Hepburn Ferrer once described his mother Audrey as "unassuming." That always strikes me as an unusual adjective for a woman who was nominated for five Academy Awards (and won the first time) and was often lavishly dressed by legendary designer Hubert de Givenchy. But, ironically, part of what has made Audrey so iconic is precisely that she lacked all semblance of pretention. As J. M. Barrie said, "Life is a long lesson in humility." And here we have our first life lesson on how to live more like Audrey.

> She always surprised people when they saw her working in the kitchen. There was absolutely nothing pretentious about her and that showed when she was preparing a meal because her tastes were so simple. She loved a good plate of pasta with tomato sauce, and her big treat was to go to hotels and order a club sandwich from room service. That made her day.
>
> —SEAN FERRER, Audrey's firstborn son

Audrey was only two years old when Albert Einstein wrote, "I believe that a simple and unassuming manner of life is best

Opposite: *Roman Holiday*, 1953

for everyone, best both for the body and the mind." It seemed that this was part of her DNA from an early age. She rose to fame on the very high heels of 1940s screen sirens, including Rita Hayworth and Lana Turner, actresses who had curvy hips and big lips and knew how to flaunt them. Part of Audrey's vast and seemingly instant appeal was that she represented something else entirely, and women around the world immediately took note. According to Pamela Keogh, one of Audrey's many biographers, "She became a role model, because she offered an alternative. It was another way of dressing, another way a woman could present herself, an acceptable and beautiful way, to the world."

> When I look at children, there's an innocence about them that hasn't been corrupted. The beauty Audrey has was quite like that.
>
> —BOB WILLOUGHBY, photographer for *Harper's Bazaar*, *Life*, and Hollywood studios like Warner Brothers

Audrey introduced the idea that women could be elegant, beautiful, and even glamorous, regardless of which body parts curved out and which curved in—and they

Opposite: *Roman Holiday*, 1953

Audrey definitely had a good heart,
there was nothing mean or petty—it's
a character thing. She had a good
character, so I think people picked up
on that, too. She didn't have any of the
backstabbing, petty gossipy personalities
that you see in this business. I liked her a
lot; in fact, I loved Audrey. It was easy to
love her.

—GREGORY PECK, American actor and
Audrey's costar in *Roman Holiday*

SCENE TAKE 5
8 21 63 70 B SC 102
'MY FAIR LADY' 877
CUKOR-STRADLING

"You take the frills away, the bows away, the 'this' away, you really see the line of something."

—Audrey

My Fair Lady, 1964

could do it without the fuss. Audrey gave it to us straight when she said, "Sex appeal is something that you feel deep down inside. It's suggested rather than shown. I'll admit that I'm not as well-stacked as Sophie Loren or Gina Lollobrigida, but there is more to sex appeal than just measurements."

> "My mother was born in 1900, very Victorian. And considered it not proper to make a spectacle of yourself, not to talk about yourself."
>
> — Audrey

Or, as British dancer, reality television star, and lifelong Audrey admirer Darcey Bussell put it, "She was always very real, one of those natural stars who never tried to be anything other than who she was. It's hard to stay true to yourself and it's rare, especially today."

Speaking of today, there is a notion, popular among life coaches and other self-help gurus, that in order to manifest and make real anything you might want in life, you must first truly believe in its attainability. If seeing is believing, then you must first

Opposite: *Breakfast at Tiffany's*, 1961

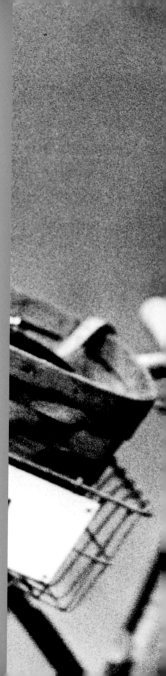

"I'm an introvert . . . I love
being by myself, love being
outdoors, love taking a
long walk with my dogs and
looking at the trees, flowers,
the sky."

—Audrey

My Fair Lady, 1964

have the opportunity to see someone else accomplish whatever it is you are seeking. After all, if some other seemingly relatable person can have it, there's no reason you can't have it, too.

> She always underdressed instead of overdressed. Nobody in the world looked better in plain white pants and a white blouse. Whatever she put on became perfectly elegant. Without a stick of jewelry, she looked like a queen.
>
> —EVA GABOR, actress

Audrey probably wouldn't have paid much attention to this notion, but for the women of her generation who weren't buxom and for whom high heels and tight dresses would have been as impractical as they were inappropriate, she was that some other relatable person. Throughout the 1950s and 1960s, she made many, many women believe they could be stylish and feel beautiful. Seeing Audrey do it meant believing you could do it, too. Seeing her succeed meant believing in your own success. The confidence and boost to morale that Audrey unwittingly gave her fans is, fortunately for you and me, just as effective today as it was decades ago.

You might not suspect it, but the key word is "unwittingly." Today, we don't have to look far to find something—practically anything—to see and then want to believe in. All those trendy life coaches, who probably would have baffled Audrey, bombard their fans with aspirational photos, quotes, listicles, recipes, and products on their blogs and Instagram accounts. Anyone with a brand or something to sell, whether a model, actress, athlete, or writer, projects a seemingly endless stream of so-called inspiration for their followers. As far as I can tell, all of this content mostly just creates more confusion and

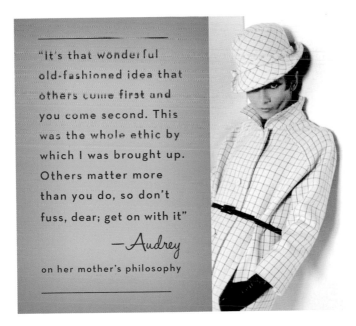

"It's that wonderful old-fashioned idea that others come first and you come second. This was the whole ethic by which I was brought up. Others matter more than you do, so don't fuss, dear; get on with it"

—*Audrey*

on her mother's philosophy

makes it difficult to judge what, if anything, is worth believing in anymore.

Even though Audrey was an actress with something to sell (her movies, ahem), she was and remains a different kind of role model—the kind that lived her life for herself and for her family. Not for Hollywood studios. Not for directors. Not for men. Not even for the work. Certainly not for any of us. I think that's why I like her so much. I think that's why she's worth believing in.

> ❝ She loved just being home with her family. We'd have dinner in the kitchen, and she loved sour apples for dessert. She certainly respected and loved her career but her family really came first. ❞
>
> —CONNIE WALD, one of Audrey's best friends, who was also a model and the wife of Hollywood producer Jerry Wald

The first museum to exhibit the work of the contemporary anonymous street artist Banksy was Moco, the Modern Contemporary Museum in Amsterdam—smack dab in the middle of Audrey territory. The exhibit included the oft quoted, "I don't know why people are so keen to put the details

"The kind of man I'm attracted to can be tall or short, fair or dark, handsome or homely. Physical good looks don't necessarily appeal to me just by themselves. If a man has the indefinable quality that I can only call 'warmth' or 'charm,' then I'll feel at ease with him."

—Audrey

Charade, 1963

of their private life in public; they forget that invisibility is a superpower." On the surface, Banksy and Audrey don't have much in common, but if you told me the artist had stolen that line from the actress, I wouldn't doubt you. Banksy and Audrey are not the only people who understand the appeal of keeping their private lives private, of course, but these days it sometimes feels that they might be.

> After so many drive-in waitresses becoming movie stars there has been this real drought, when along comes class: somebody who actually went to school, can spell, maybe even plays the piano. She may be a wispy, thin little thing, but when you see that girl you know you're really in the presence of something: in that league there's only ever been Garbo, and the other Hepburn, and maybe Bergman: it's a rare quality, but boy, do you know when you've found it.
>
> —BILLY WILDER, screenwriter and director

Opposite: *The Children's Hour*, 1961

> *She never really moved to Hollywood. Not the place, not the state of mind.*
>
> —**SEAN FERRER**, Audrey's firstborn son

> " She used to surprise my friends with how casual she was. They expected something incredible and instead found just a nice person. "
>
> —LUCA DOTTI, Audrey's younger son

What sets Audrey apart from the private citizens who live quiet, offline lives, and even from Banksy, whose career is supported by, not hindered by, his anonymity, is that she was an actress. Not a theatrical actress or an avant-garde actress but first and foremost a Hollywood film actress, who made her living entirely on the screen, not the screen of our phones or computers, but the biggest screen of all time. It was different for actors, especially then, many of whom could get away with an elusive John Wayne–style silence or a slippery Cary Grant–style mysteriousness, and it only made them that much more alluring. For actresses like Audrey, however, beautiful women who depended on success in front of the camera, invisibility was not a superpower; it was the kiss of death.

As true as that was then, it is even truer now. That's the prevailing theory, anyway, and that certainly was and continues to be the great fear. But Audrey paid it all no mind. She bucked that perception so gracefully, so sweetly, so unassumingly, that

"I lack self-confidence. I don't know whether I shall ever get it. Perhaps it is better to be unsure of yourself, as I am. But it is very tiring."

—Audrey

> "Her enormous potential cinema success, with attendant salary, seems to have made little impression on this delightful human being. She appears to take her wholesale adulation with a pinch of salt, and gratitude rather than puffed up pride. Everything is very simple around her: no maid to help her dress or answer the door to guests. In a flash, I discovered she is chock-a-block with sprite-like charm, and she has a sort of waifish, poignant sympathy. Without any preliminaries, she cuts through to a basic understanding that makes people friends: nothing has to be explained, we like each other. A chord had been struck and I knew that the next time we met we would continue straight from here with no recapitulation of formalities: this was a unique occasion."
>
> —CECIL BEATON, fashion photographer and designer

no one in Hollywood seems to have realized what she was up to, and by the time they understood and might have thought to

Love in the Afternoon, 1957

> "As you get older, it's nice to feel you belong somewhere—having lived a rather circus life."
>
> *—Audrey*

protest, she was legendary, box office gold. No one was going to complain then. This side of Audrey might be my very favorite side of hers—the cheeky, do whatever she wants side, done so smoothly and so successfully that no one else remembers she's actually gone and done exactly what they thought they didn't want her to do. That's the real power of the unassuming.

When we think about actresses, we usually think of them in the spotlight. But that is only one small part of what it means to act. It's not anywhere near the whole of the work. Audrey understood this. The stage is the sharing part, which is a gorgeous gift, but first you have to have something to share. You don't win the Academy Award for Best Actress at the age of twenty-four by accident. Audrey spent most of her time letting other people talk and letting other people move and be. And not just any people, but people she loved and respected and could learn from. Only when she had something to offer, did she take the stage. The real work of acting and creating came offstage.

When you are unassuming like Audrey, you have the great privilege and the great power to move through life ruffling the world's feathers only if and when you want to or need to. You have the extraordinary ability to listen and to observe and to learn from people when they have the most to teach—that is, when they think they are unobserved. 👓

Paris When It Sizzles, 1964

Chapter 2

THE ART OF BEING GRACIOUS

"The greatest victory in my life has been to be able to live with myself, to accept my shortcomings and those of others. I'm a long way from being the human being I'd like to be. But I've decided I'm not so bad after all."

—*Audrey*

Funny Face, 1957

"I'm truly, truly grateful and terribly happy."

— *Audrey*

winning the best actress Oscar for *Roman Holiday*

T o no one's surprise, I have never met Vanessa Redgrave. So I do not recall when or how I realized she was tall and strong, but it must have been many years ago, as a child even, because I cannot remember a time when I did not think of her as an Amazon woman. I mean that literally, by the way, not insultingly. I think of her as one of the Amazon woman warriors in Greek mythology, Hippolyta's best friend, let's say. Vanessa is six feet tall, and, unlike today's popular fashion models, her stance is solid, firm. She doesn't move unless she wants to, and when she was very young, she wanted to move as a dancer. In fact, she was an aspiring ballerina. If you've ever watched her glide across a stage or a screen, this will not surprise you.

> A great [wo]man is always willing to be little.
>
> —RALPH WALDO EMERSON

Vanessa trained at Audrey's dance academy in London, before they both got too tall for the ballet and had to settle for their plan B, acting. Despite being a few years younger than Audrey, Vanessa remembers "what a lovely looking, vivacious, friendly face" the older student had. By the time Vanessa laced

Sabrina, 1954

up her ballet slippers and stepped up to the barre, Audrey had been in London long enough to catch the attention of the city's cabaret directors. These professional castings impressed her classmates. Audrey's theatrical roles and, eventually, the small British film parts that followed ("ciggy girl #1") were widely discussed among her peers. But, according to Vanessa, "she was very, very humble." I'd like to see Vanessa and Audrey try to out-humble each other—both would almost certainly insist the other had won.

> 66 It wasn't just rolling out some old legend. It was an honor to be there [on set with Audrey]. And an honor to be in her presence. 99
>
> —RICHARD DREYFUSS, American actor and Audrey's costar in *Always*

Many, many people have recognized Audrey's striking humility over the years, but Vanessa may well have been one of the first to identify it. I guess it takes one to know one. What exactly does it mean to be humble? In one sense, and certainly for our purposes in better understanding Audrey and how we might emulate her, humility is the power of invisibility

“ She had not gone to acting school. She didn't hear the word Strasberg. She did not repeat in front of a mirror. She just was born with this kind of quality. And she made it look so unforced, so simple, so easy . . . she wasn't playing the Oscar winner [after her win for *Roman Holiday*, while filming *Sabrina*]. She was humble. ”

—**BILLY WILDER**, screenwriter and director

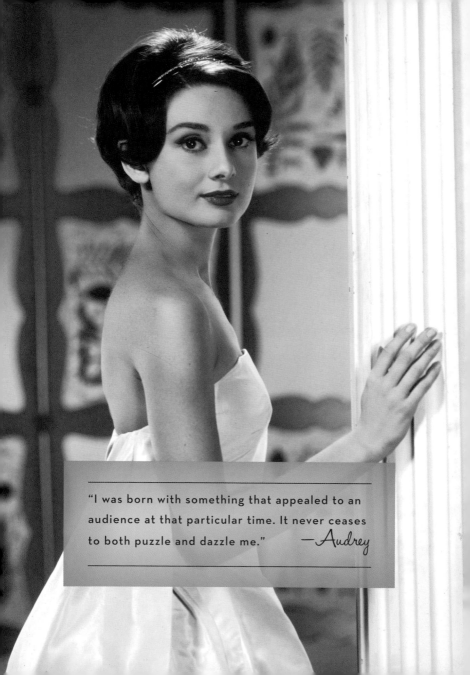

"I was born with something that appealed to an audience at that particular time. It never ceases to both puzzle and dazzle me." —Audrey

writ large, but it is so much more than choosing to be quiet or choosing to disappear in the crowd when it "Hubert de Givenchy" suits you. At its most rudimentary, humility is simply the lack of pretension. But this definition still seems incomplete, and I've never much liked to define things by what they lack. Humility really stems from an abundance of respect; respect for yourself, for other people, and for situations, especially when the person or the situation is unpleasant or difficult. Audrey always had enough respect for others and the larger world to understand that you are not always the guest of honor even if sometimes you get to be the life of the party.

> She was born modest. When she talked about getting an award, getting good reviews, she will always bring up the help that she got.
>
> —BILLY WILDER, screenwriter and director

And what then is respect? I'm talking about giving it, not receiving it. Respect outclasses the letter of the law. It is more nuanced than a fact on a page. It has the sophistication and the wisdom to take under consideration as many aspects of a situation as possible and to subsequently arrive at an

Breakfast at Tiffany's, 1961

"Anyone who ever gave you confidence, you owe them a lot."

—*Audrey*

as Holly Golightly in *Breakfast at Tiffany's*

appropriate behavior, at a way forward, that is both sensitive and inclusive. In other words, respect is thoughtfulness, and when you give it consciously and with great care, you embody graciousness and earn respect. You reap what you sow. Audrey's nuanced grasp of these distinctions and their significance is what gave her grace and made her graciousness not only genuine but also unforgettable.

And so we come to our next life lesson from Audrey, which the early twentieth-century actress, designer, and writer Elsie De Wolfe famously summarized as, "Be pretty if you can, be witty if you must, but be gracious if it kills you."

> "You can tell more about a person by what he says about others than you can by what others say about him."
>
> —Audrey

Of all the many distinguished and esteemed qualities that Audrey embodied and for which she is deservedly remembered and celebrated, her graciousness may be the most worthy of examination and emulation. She had an extraordinary gift for

it. A Swedish journalist once interviewed Audrey in a park in Stockholm and was struck by a particular moment: "Without thinking, Audrey jumped out on the rock, so we could get a better picture, and I am sure she would have just laughed if she had fallen in the water." You may not associate jumping on rocks with graciousness, but it is exactly that if you are Audrey Hepburn and you want to help a journalist get a better story. What a thought—an actress helping the paparazzi. When Hubert de Givenchy said that Audrey "was an enchantress, inspiring love and beauty," he was referring to her gorgeous generosity of spirit.

> "I didn't know what I was doing. I acted instinctively. And had one of the greatest schools of all, a whole row of great, great directors."
>
> —Audrey

Predictably, however, that is not quite how Audrey saw herself. At least, not according to her younger son, Luca Dotti, who told a reporter, "My mother didn't think she was generous. She would think, 'I can do it, therefore I must do it.'

Opposite: *How to Steal a Million*, 1966

Breakfast at Tiffany's, 1961

"My greatest ambition is to have a career without becoming a career woman."

—Audrey

She understood how famous she was and that her fame could be used in a nice way. What she always said was that she, like everybody, would tend to be a little bit lazy, because we are all into our lives. But if you mix [your] message into something more important, it can really make a difference."

And yet, somehow, despite all of her energy and her extraordinary empathy, she remained quite simply Audrey. "People thought it couldn't be normal to be living with Audrey Hepburn, but there was no secret cave where she wore a little black dress," said Luca. The same sentiment is more striking and revelatory coming from a friend. "After five minutes with Audrey you forgot who she was for everybody else," her long-time friend Anna Cataldi once said.

How did Audrey manage to always strike the right note, no matter where she was or with whom she was keeping company? Her secret may have been in her understanding of balance and moderation and in knowing herself and listening to herself. "I have to be alone very often. I'd be quite happy if I spent from Saturday night until Monday morning alone in my apartment. That's how I refuel." She understood that the sensitivity and awareness necessary to constantly tap into what others are thinking and feeling and needing is draining and demands routine periods of rest. Little wonder then that her private space and home came to mean so much to her. As her friend for many decades Connie Wald put it, "[Her home in Switzerland] was just a haven for her, all in white and the gardens were just so beautiful and the trees and the walks with the dogs and everything wonderful there." Respect the rest you need, but, also, seek your restoration in a place that makes you

Breakfast at Tiffany's, 1961

Charade, 1963

Roman Holiday, 1953

feel good, surrounded by as much natural beauty as you can—
and, yes, bodega flowers totally count.

On more than one occasion Audrey said that she was
"born with an enormous need for affection and a terrible need
to give it." Perhaps this is where some of her graciousness came

"I owe Greg [Peck] a great deal, because stars had approval of costars or co-actors."

—Audrey

from and why and how it came to be such a crucial part of the way she lived. When Audrey said this, she was essentially describing the Golden Rule as it applied to her own life. Maybe, sometimes, it really is as simple as that: Give affection recklessly. Take affection graciously. Rest. Repeat. ●●

THE AUTHENTICITY OF BEING STYLISH

"I created a look, in order to make something of myself."

—Audrey

My Fair Lady, 1964

A udrey once famously claimed, "My look is attainable. Women can look like Audrey Hepburn by flipping out their hair, buying the large sunglasses, and the little sleeveless dresses." For a person who got so very much exactly right, Audrey is sadly mistaken on this account. Looking like her is not nearly as attainable as she suggested if you haven't been born with that swan-like neck or those saucer-like eyes, warm and dark as a cup of strong coffee. And even if the gods did bless you with those same dramatic features, they aren't enough, I'm sorry to report. Because Audrey's exquisite fashion style was ultimately only a token reflection of her even more beautiful character.

> 66 Audrey had exquisite taste. She and her mother had no money, but they had class and style. Audrey used to go to department stores in Amsterdam and buy plain-looking hats and with her artistic talent, easily change them into something really nice. 99
>
> —LOEKIE VAN OVEN, a Gaskell dancer who took Audrey under her wing after the war

Opposite: *Breakfast at Tiffany's*, 1961

Still, we can fake it 'til we make it, right?

After all, even Audrey wasn't born looking like Princess Ann in *Roman Holiday* or Nicole, the chic wealthy French girl in *How to Steal a Million*. Years before a twenty-four-year-old Audrey would finish filming *Roman Holiday* and fly to Paris to introduce herself to Hubert de Givenchy, she spent her adolescence and early adulthood in clothes that either she or her mother had sewn. During the war, of course, this had been a necessity not only for her family but also for most everyone in the Netherlands under the Occupation. In the lean years after the war as well, when Audrey and her mother lived in a one-room flat and she performed every night in the London cabarets and walked home in the earliest morning hours through the throng of Piccadilly Circus prostitutes, she continued to wear the simple homemade clothes she knew how to make and that fit her budget.

> "I always dreamt of the day I would have enough closets—big ones. Some people dream of having a big swimming pool, with me it is closets."
>
> —Audrey

> For me her charm lay not in the androgyny
> of simple hair and a boyish figure, but
> in a style that seemed the embodiment
> of sophisticated, existential Europe as
> opposed to the overripe artificiality of
> Hollywood.
>
> ELIZABETH WILSON, in Britain's *Sight and
> Sound* and as quoted by Barry Paris in his
> biography *Audrey Hepburn*

Funny Face, 1957

Sketches by Hubert de Givenchy of Audrey's costumes for *Charade*. Givenchy designed outfits for Audrey for six of her films.

And though it may not have been apparent from her dress in those days, she spent those years paying very close attention to fashion. So much so, in fact, that when she was cast in *Sabrina* as a young, unsophisticated chauffeur's daughter who returns from studying the culinary arts in Paris utterly transformed by the designer fashions she discovered abroad, it was Audrey's idea that the twenty-six-year-old Hubert de Givenchy should design her costumes. Even then, she knew her Parisian designers, especially the ones she could relate to—the young, up-and-coming ones.

> "Givenchy's creations always gave me a sense of security and confidence, and my work went more easily in the knowledge that I looked absolutely right. I felt the same at my private appearances. Givenchy's outfits gave me 'protection' against strange situations and people. I felt so good in them."
>
> —Audrey

Sabrina director Billy Wilder had already enlisted Paramount's wardrobe supervisor, Edith Head, to design the elaborate outfits of Sabrina Fairchild, but after meeting with Head in San Francisco, Audrey came up with the Givenchy idea and managed to sell Wilder on it, too. She may have been very young and walking around in very basic hand-stitched frocks, but Audrey was no rube. Who wouldn't want to wear designer clothes, especially on a movie studio's dime? Audrey certainly did, and she knew how to orchestrate it, too.

Still, even de Givenchy underestimated her at first—partly to blame is the fact that he had assumed the "Miss Hepburn" he was to meet was Katharine. Even though Audrey had already finished filming *Roman Holiday*, she was still a complete unknown. Instead of Katharine, Givenchy remembers "this very thin person with beautiful eyes, short hair,

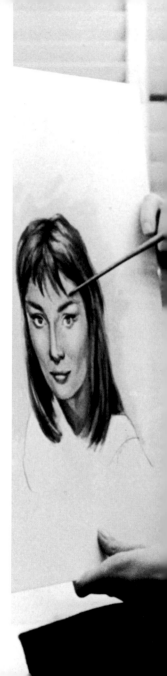

Charade, 1963

thick eyebrows, very tiny trousers, ballerina shoes, and a little T-shirt. On her head was a straw gondolier's hat with a red ribbon around it that said VENEZIA. I thought, 'This is too much!'"

French fashion doyenne Dreda Mele, who was also there at that moment, described Audrey as looking "like the arrival of a summer flower. She was lumineuse—radiant, in both a physical and spiritual sense. I felt immediately how lovely she was, inside and out. Though she came to Givenchy out of the blue, there is no doubt that they were made to meet.

> "Everyone has his own style. When you have found it, you should stick to it."
>
> —Audrey

"Audrey was always very definite in her taste and look. She came to him because she was attracted by the image he could give her. And she entered that image totally. She entered into his dream, too. I repeat; they were made for each other." Little wonder then that, many years later, Givenchy would refer to his lifelong friendship with Audrey as "a kind of marriage."

Their meeting was not only the beginning of their personal friendship, but it also came at the beginning of both of their careers, which would forever after be intertwined. "I can't think of any other picture before *Sabrina* that made use of clothes in the same way. It was a real breakthrough. The way Audrey looked in *Sabrina* had an effect on the roles she later played. It's fair to say that if she had never gone to Paris [and

Two for the Road, 1967

met Givenchy] she wouldn't have had that role in *Breakfast at Tiffany's*. The *Sabrina* clothes fixed her image forever," said Ernest Lehman, who along with Billy Wilder and Samuel Taylor, wrote the screenplay for *Sabrina*.

---

66 Audrey was always more about fashion than movies or acting. 99

—STANLEY DONEN, director and choreographer

The first lesson from that fateful day emerged only when Audrey began to try on the designer's clothes. "The change from the little girl who arrived that morning was unbelievable . . . She gave a life to the clothes. She had a way of installing herself in them that I have seen in no one else since, except maybe the model Dalma. The suit just adapted to her. Something magic happened," de Givenchy remembered. Audrey wasn't just meeting a talented designer; she was finding her signature style. Everyone, no matter what they look like or what they can afford, has a style that will bring out the best in them. The challenge, of course, is finding that style. Audrey was fortunate to find it early.

The second lesson came when Audrey began to accessorize de Givenchy's designs. "Audrey always added a twist, something

"Clothes are positively a passion with me. I love them to the point where it is practically a vice."

—Audrey

piquant, amusing, to the clothes. Though of course I advised her, she knew precisely what she wanted," de Givenchy said.

And how did she know what she wanted?

Quite simply, she knew what looked good on her. She knew style wasn't about trends—she would have looked absurd in the fashions fancied by the likes of Jayne Mansfield and Elizabeth Taylor. So she didn't bother trying. When Edith Head told her she ought to stay away from "dead black," Audrey followed her own fashion instincts and focused on what she knew flattered her, including the sleek, shiny black cocktail dress with the delicate shoulder ties in *Sabrina*, the vivid black lace number and matching mask that she wore in *How to Steal a Million*, and, of course, most iconically of all, the black dress and gloves she wore in *Breakfast at Tiffany's*. As de Givenchy described it, "She knew herself very well. For example, which is her good profile and which is her bad. She was very professional. No detail ever escaped her."

Far more important than how well suited Audrey was for designer clothing was the simplicity of Audrey's approach to dressing throughout her life. She understood innately what most of us have to learn the hard way: that simple doesn't have to mean boring and that elaborate doesn't always mean stylish. Her son Luca has repeatedly said that his mother's favorite

Opposite: *Charade*, 1963

Charade, 1963

"I've got to do something about the way I look. I mean a girl just can't go to Sing Sing with a green face."

— *Audrey*

as Holly Golightly in *Breakfast at Tiffany's*

color was cyan, which is a rich, bright, blue-green shade that manages to be both elegant and cheery, calm, never showy, never ostentatious. (Now, who does that remind you of?) It was a color that frequently showed up in her home in Switzerland, from the linens on her bed to the shutters on the windows. And, of course, it's also the shade of blue synonymous with a certain jewelry store on Fifth Avenue, where Holly Golightly would go for calm, because she said, "The quietness and the proud look of it; nothing very bad could happen to you there. If I could find a real-life place that'd make me feel like Tiffany's, then . . . then I'd buy some furniture and give the cat a name!"

The way Audrey thought a home should look and feel is exactly how she kept her appearance. She lived by the timeless adage "quality not quantity." As Audrey's friend Jean Bayless,

Opposite: *My Fair Lady*, 1964

"It's having the best of both worlds, Hubert (de Givenchy) and Ralph (Lauren). I don't want to compare them. I just want to wear them."

—Audrey

who costarred with her in Cecil Landau's *Sauce Tartare* and *Sauce Piquante* in London, told it, "We all got a £20 salary, and she bought two coats with her £20, two coats for £10 each from Austin Reed. She bought a black, and she bought a grey. And I bought a little plastic handbag. She did not approve and tried to teach me to have a little more taste."

> ❝ Whether Audrey was in jeans and a bandana or all dolled up for the Oscars— she was so beautiful that you couldn't bear it. ❞ —ANDRÉ PREVIN, composer

Whether it was a sheath dress or a bateau top, a pair of cropped black pants or a pair of ballet flats, Audrey knew how to make a statement that looked effortless. It was not effortless in the slightest, of course, but the reason it appeared to be was because nothing was complicated or confusing. The parts were simple: excellent quality, cuts that flattered her figure, and clothing one could wear to hop on a Vespa, take a brisk walk through the woods, eat a croissant, pick up a puppy, and dance, always dance. Taken together, these parts equaled something more; they equaled Audrey. And they can equal you, too. 👓

Opposite: *Funny Face*, 1957

Chapter 4

THE VIRTUE
OF BEING
FUNNY

"It's useful being top banana
in the shock department."

—*Audrey*

as Holly Golightly in
Breakfast at Tiffany's

How to Steal a Million, 1966

owadays, the kind of humor we may encounter in romantic comedies or standup specials can be quite crass and cynical. Even some of our most lauded female comedians, the ones who are breaking down gender barriers, use this type of humor when they step up to the microphone. This can be entertaining, but it's only a sliver of what it means to be funny. Like everything else she did, Audrey demonstrated a timeless and gracious approach to comedy.

> Most people think of Audrey Hepburn as regal. I like to think of her as spunky . . . she was a cutup; she was a clown. I think that would surprise people who didn't know her. She could always make me laugh between scenes . . . she was a comic.
>
> —GREGORY PECK, American actor and Audrey's costar in *Roman Holiday*

Fortunately for us, Audrey's style of comedy bears a striking resemblance to her style of dress. Consistent as ever, when it came to being a funny lady, she was a lot more than just a funny face. She wasn't crass, and she was never a cynic, as she herself made plain when she said, "The world has always been cynical, and I think I'm a romantic at heart. I hope for better things, and I thank God the world is also full of people who want to be genuine and kind."

> She was happiest not wearing makeup and at home with the dogs and the flowers and giggling away or going to the movies, not being a movie star at all.
>
> —DORIS BRYNNER, model and the wife of actor Yul Brynner

Comedians and performers often point to a difficult stage in their childhood that made them turn to humor. Perhaps they told jokes to diffuse tension between their parents or to mask pain they themselves were feeling. When sarcasm persists in our culture, we have a tendency to think that humor and sincerity are incompatible. But the proof against this is Audrey. Her humor came from her kindness, her generosity, and her joy—not in spite of them.

She was eager to smile and to make people happy, so eager that she didn't wait around for somebody else to make her laugh or to put the room at ease. She would happily do it

Opposite: *My Fair Lady*, 1964

herself, if she had to (and she always thought she had to). Of course, it was easier for the physically adept Audrey, because all it took was an unexpected pirouette, a cartwheel, or a funny fling of that long graceful neck to make others laugh.

> Audrey and I decided we'd throw a party for the cast and the crew when the picture was finished. We went all out, had it catered by Romanoff's—nothing but the best. In the middle of the party, Audrey sidled up to me, jabbed me with her elbow and said, out of the corner of her mouth, 'Hey, Shirl-Girl, whattya think the bruise is gonna be for this bash?
>
> —SHIRLEY MACLAINE,
> Audrey's costar in *The Children's Hour*

Audrey's hard work and discipline are well documented, but that doesn't mean she was serious all the time. She didn't shy away from joking around behind the camera with the rest of the cast and the crew. She knew that part of working hard means knowing how to collaborate and how to make it easier for the entire cast and crew to be successful. Making the work

Opposite: *Two for the Road*, 1967

Paris When It Sizzles, 1964

"I didn't expect anything much and because of that I'm the least bitter woman I know."

—Audrey

fun is part of the job. Every time Audrey started a new movie, she understood that she was partly responsible for ensuring that the mood on set was positive.

---

6 6 She was love and humor and grace and opening and knowing. She was perfect. 9 9

—RICHARD DREYFUSS,
American actor and Audrey's costar in *Always*

When she began filming *How to Steal a Million* with Peter O'Toole in the mid-1960s, at the very height of her international fame, Audrey was not in a good place personally. Now more than a decade into her first marriage with Mel Ferrer, the relationship was unraveling and was not helped when Audrey suffered another miscarriage. Still, she refused to let her personal pain get in the way of the movie or in the way of her great pleasure in working alongside the warm and very funny O'Toole.

One late night of filming left a particularly strong impression on O'Toole, who recalled the evening's activities in several different interviews over the course of many years. "We were filming an exterior in Paris," he said, "and the weather

Opposite: *Breakfast at Tiffany's*, 1961

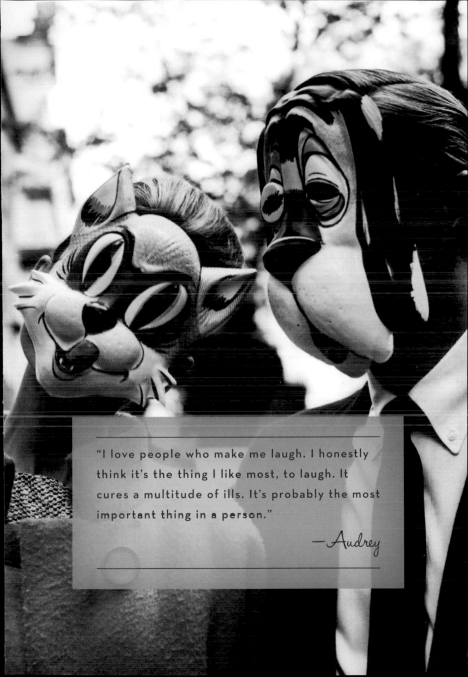

"I love people who make me laugh. I honestly think it's the thing I like most, to laugh. It cures a multitude of ills. It's probably the most important thing in a person."

—Audrey

How to Steal a Million, 1966

turned round and became very, very cold indeed. Audrey had to walk across the street, get into a waiting car and drive off, but the poor child had turned bright blue with cold. The light was going, and the shot was needed. I pulled Audrey into the caravan and gave her a shot of brandy and soda. She went all roses and cream, bounced out of the caravan, radiated towards the motor car, hopped into it and drove off, taking with her five great big lamps [being used to light the scene], the trimmers of which had flung themselves on the cobbles out of the way.

> " Hepburn is as fresh and frisky as a puppy out of the tub: she brings a candid innocence and tomboy intelligence to a part that might have gone sticky, and her performance comes like a breath of fresh air in a stifling season. "
>
> —THE NEW YORK HERALD TRIBUNE
> on Audrey in *Gigi*

"So I told her the story of Sir Edmund Kean [the nineteenth-century stage actor], who went on stage a bit drunk one day [when he was playing the part of Richard III in *Richard III*]. The audience shouted, 'Boo, you're drunk.' And

"Anyone who does not believe in miracles is not a realist."

— Audrey

Edmund Kean said, 'If you think I am drunk, wait till you see the Duke of Buckingham.' From then on she was my Duke of Buckingham." At the end of filming, Audrey gave O'Toole a parting gift, a copy of Milton's *Paradise Lost*. She signed it the "Duke of Buckingham."

Yes, she could be incredibly witty and charming when she was taking a break on the set with her costars or when she was relaxing with her friends at home between movies. But Audrey could be very funny when the camera started rolling, too. And not just in *Funny Face*. In fact, *Funny Face* almost least of all. Anneke van Wijk, who was friends with Audrey when they were teenagers and took dance lessons together, told one of Audrey's biographers that the Audrey she remembered was spontaneous and funny, qualities that her natural physicality surely enhanced and made all the more memorable. "Audrey's expression was fabulous. The way she used her hands and

How to Steal a Million, 1966

eyes showed that she also had talent for acting," Anneke said. "Her enormous eyes were not to be believed. I asked her once, 'What are you doing to make them seem so wide?' She said, 'Nothing. They've always been this way.'" When a director yelled, "Action!" Audrey put those hands and eyes to work and, more often than not, did so for comedic effect.

> *Audrey was unique. She had a kind of joyous nature. She was funny and she was dear and she was disciplined. She was a hard worker. And yet you always felt comfortable because she made it easy. The camera loved her. There was no way you could photograph her badly. She just glowed when the camera started.*
>
> —BLAKE EDWARDS,
> director of *Breakfast at Tiffany's*

The first five films Audrey appeared in were comedies. Over the course of her career, she would act in a total of twenty-seven films, eighteen of which were comedies or romantic comedies. Anyone who has seen *Wait Until Dark* knows Audrey was more than capable of great dramatic depth in the

Opposite: *Paris When It Sizzles*, 1964

How to Steal a Million, 1966

parts she took on, but she much more frequently found herself acting in lighter fare. She had the intrinsic whimsy, sparkly eyes, and big grin to pull off characters that teetered between savvy and frothy, and she was never afraid to dance, jump, or twist—whatever the role called for. "She was a pixie. You didn't know when she'd suddenly climb a tree or hurdle a hedge or just vanish in a spiral of smoke," as a friend of Audrey's once put it to her biographer Barry Paris.

> "I can think of a dozen men who are just longing to use my shower."
>
> —*Audrey* as Reggie Lampert in *Charade*

More impressive still, her gift for and frequent employ of physical comedy never diminished her dignity or her reputation among her fans. Her background as a dancer gave her a knack for effortlessly capturing a loose-limbed kind of comedy, all the while maintaining grace and elegance. As screenwriter N. T. Binh once wrote, "Audrey Hepburn is the only comedienne capable of brushing her teeth while still maintaining her glamour." Whether she was playing hooky with Gregory Peck, playing coy

Opposite: *Two for the Road*, 1967

with Peter O'Toole, or playing games with Cary Grant, Audrey knew how to give a performance that incorporated a kick, a wink, and, always, a heart.

---

66 She had no lines to say, no part to play: but with her infectious grin and her bouncing enthusiasm she actually looked as if she were enjoying herself. Perhaps it was this marked contrast with what the rest of us were feeling that made her as conspicuous as a fresh carnation on a shabby suit. 99

—MILTON SHULMA, theater and film critic, on Audrey's early work in the London theater and cabaret

---

She understood that cynicism and bitterness don't make you smarter or better. Instead, they make you and the things you want to do harder. She was not afraid of looking silly, nor was she afraid of being happy, which is a rarer sentiment than you might think. She understood that nobody else was responsible for showing her a good time and that the only way she could ensure joy was to create it for herself and then share the hell out of it. This is another lesson we can take from Audrey's playbook.

Roman Holiday, 1953

" I thought uppermost she was a delightful romantic comedienne . . . Whatever she did was so delightful that one was happy to watch her. "

— French actress **LESLIE CARON**

Chapter 5

THE GRACE OF BEING STRONG

"I did *War and Peace* in velvet and fur in August. In the hunting scene the horse fainted. They say I'm strong as a horse. I'm stronger!"

—*Audrey*

Charade, 1963

ragile. Vulnerable. Someone you want to protect. These are words and sentiments that fans and writers have repeatedly expressed about Audrey with such consistency that they are now seamlessly interwoven into our official Audrey narrative. There is considerable truth in them. This is partially because we are all fragile, we are all vulnerable, and we all need protection. But they are also true because of who Audrey was.

> Her personal style was a result of her unwillingness to compromise on these values and to focus on what is basic and real. She showed a great deal of stubbornness to outside influences, always insisting on what felt natural and comfortable. Her sense of appropriateness and decorum was happily mixed with a sense of irony and humor— not taking herself too seriously but seriously enough.
>
> —ROBERT WOLDERS, Audrey's significant other and partner for the last several years of her life

After all, Katharine Hepburn was one of us, too, but we don't think of frailty when we consider *that* Hepburn. With Audrey, however, you only need one glance to see the vast expanse of vulnerability she carried. Her physical slightness made her appear breakable, and her big eyes brought her emotions so close to the surface they looked forever in danger of spilling over. Part of the reason we have linked Audrey to delicacy is because she encouraged us to do so, which is a testament to her professional shrewdness, her acting ability, and her choice of characters. We know this because the people who worked with her and who came to know her best tell us how struck they were by her grit and her personal power. They speak about her strength as often as they speak about her vulnerability, because, like her fans, they didn't expect it. They didn't see the full force of Audrey coming.

> 66 Audrey was never bothered by the physical hardships of making a picture. 99
>
> —MEL FERRER, Audrey's first husband

Her son Sean once told a reporter, "When she came into a room, all eyes were on her. She could be silly and frivolous, but she had a strong sense of personal boundaries, and people

❝ I never saw anyone work so hard. She was tireless in learning both the songs and the dances. It wasn't like Cyd Charisse or Ginger Rogers, who did it all the time. Roger Edens would say, 'Audrey, take tomorrow off. You've been working sixteen hours a day.' She'd say, 'No, I'll be here at nine.' And then she'd be there at eight. ❞

—LEONARD GERSHE, screenwriter of *Funny Face*

just knew not to take advantage of her graciousness. I never saw anyone misbehave in her presence. It just wasn't done." Audrey, you may be surprised to learn, was not in the habit of taking anybody's nonsense. She was just always very polite about turning it down.

My Fair Lady, 1964

> She was a living embodiment of the best of the human heart, the human mind, and soul. And I think people drew sustenance from that.

—HARRY BELAFONTE, American singer, actor, and activist

Audrey may have been born looking like a fine princess, but her childhood had given her a resiliency and a resolve that most people take a lifetime to develop, if they have the fortitude to develop it at all. She was not innocent. She was not naive. She told her sons that during the war, when she was just eleven years old, she carried messages for the Dutch Resistance in her shoes. The war, coinciding as it did with the end of her childhood and beginning of her adolescence, made her first vulnerable and then strong. The same can be said about the almost unfathomable international fame she achieved at the end of her adolescence and the beginning of her adulthood, which made her first more vulnerable and then stronger than ever. Most of us have some combination of strength and vulnerability, but we don't always know how to use them together or separately to our advantage. Audrey knew how to turn her vulnerability into strength.

You know you're strong and adroit when you can talk about something incredibly difficult and painful and still be coquettish about it. In 1953, Audrey flew to Los Angeles to complete a screen test as part of her audition for the role of Princess Ann in *Roman Holiday*. The twenty-four-year-old had never been to California and had yet to star in any movie. During the film test, the casting director asked Audrey about the secret dance recitals she had given in Holland during the war, which the Germans had forbidden. Audrey replied, "In about 1944, about a year before the end of the war, I was quite capable of performing, and [the recitals were] a sort of, some way, in which I could make some contribution. And I did give performances to collect money for the underground, which always needed money." Next, the casting director asked, "And what about the Germans, how did they feel about it?" Without missing a beat, Audrey answered, "They didn't know about it." Better still, she had barely finished the sentence when she proceeded to break into an unabashed grin. That's what Audrey's kind of strength looks like: moxie. And that's how you win the starring role of princess in a major Hollywood movie as a complete unknown.

There's been a fair amount of discussion about the roles that Audrey played, starting with Princess Ann. What do *Roman Holiday*, *Sabrina*, *War and Peace*, *Love in the Afternoon*,

Opposite: *Breakfast at Tiffany's*, 1961

"I don't believe in collective guilt, but I do believe in collective responsibility."

—Audrey

Funny Face, *The Nun's Story*, *The Unforgiven*, *Charade*, *Paris When It Sizzles*, *My Fair Lady*, and *How to Steal a Million* all have in common? In each, Audrey was paired with a leading man who was significantly older. Some critics have argued that films such as *Love in the Afternoon*, *Funny Face*, and *Paris When It Sizzles* did poorly at the box office precisely because of the May-December romances at their centers. In response, Audrey told a reporter at the *New York World Telegram*, "The charge is particularly unfair to Coop [Gary Cooper]. In *Love in the Afternoon* he's not trying to fool anyone. He's supposed to be a man of fifty. That's the whole point of the story. As for Fred Astaire, who cares how old he is? He's Fred Astaire! If anyone doesn't like it, he can go jump in the lake." (Remember what we said earlier about Audrey not taking anybody's nonsense?)

66 She played the younger lady to the older man several times in movies, and I think it was believable, because she had a maturity. People say she was vulnerable, but yet she had confidence. She had such self-confidence in what she was doing that she made all of these relationships work. 99

—**HENRY MANCINI**, lyricist who wrote "Moon River" for Audrey Hepburn and *Breakfast at Tiffany's*

Sabrina, 1954

"No, people don't belong to people. I'll never let anyone put me in a cage."

—*Audrey*

as Holly Golightly in *Breakfast at Tiffany's*

Charade, 1963

> I've never seen anybody change so much in front of a camera as Audrey. In life, you'd think, 'How is she going to get through the day or even the hour?' Her hands were shaking, she's smoking too much, she's worried, she's being kind of desperately nice to everybody, she's so fragile . . . But between the time she stepped in front of the camera and you said, 'Action!,' something happened. She pulled it together. A kind of strength through vulnerability—strength like an iron butterfly . . . The performance was true, never weak, always strong and clear. It was an amazing thing to watch, this professional completely in charge of her instrument without even thinking about it. I think it was all second nature.

—PETER BOGDANOVICH,

who directed Audrey in the film *They All Laughed*

Whether or not these couplings worked or didn't and regardless of whether or not audiences cared, why was Audrey so rarely paired with someone her own age? Without question, part of the answer has nothing to do with Audrey at all. Don't forget, this is Hollywood we're talking about. Old men are forever getting the girl while old women get to play the girl's mother, if they get cast at all. The problem, and it is a problem, persists (think *Lost in Translation*, *Magic in the Moonlight*, *Black Swan*, every Jack Nicholson movie ever made).

On the other hand and also without question, part of the answer has absolutely everything to do with Audrey. Was it because she was so vulnerable she needed to be cast opposite a strong, older actor who could help prop her up? *Hardly*. For an actress who made fewer than thirty films, it is notable that Audrey managed to headline alongside twelve of the finest actors of the twentieth century: Gregory Peck, Humphrey Bogart, Henry Fonda, Mel Ferrer, Gary Cooper, Fred Astaire, Peter Finch, Burt Lancaster, Cary Grant, William Holden, Rex Harrison, and Peter O'Toole. Perhaps the real reason she found herself so often in the onscreen company of older men is because it took a more experienced actor to match Audrey's strength as an actress and on camera presence. Your feelings about each of the twelve men on Audrey's list may vary, but, undoubtedly, they were all strong. Just not as strong as Audrey.

That does not mean, however, that Audrey's strength is unattainable. We know that in childhood and for many years

Audrey sensed very early in her life and career that self-worth based on fame or beauty is very short-lived, and so she remained forever herself—realistic, aware, and caring. —ROBERT WOLDERS, Audrey's significant other and partner for the last several years of her life

Wait Until Dark, 1967

into her young adulthood, Audrey sewed her own outfits. She sewed pants, shirts, and jackets in the style of the trends she could not afford, and that's about what a lot of us think of when we think about sewing: cute clothes. But Audrey knew more, something many of us forget: the strength of a stitch. And we don't rely on sewing for just fashion but for safety equipment like seatbelts and parachutes, too. It can take hundreds of pounds of force to tear apart the stitches of nylon thread sewn into a straight seam. And remember, too, the dancing Audrey did all those years while she was sewing her clothes—it takes a lot of strength to be a ballerina, light on her feet. You've seen *Black Swan*. You've taken a barre class. You know.

> She knew exactly how to shape her strong, independent image. This naturally extended to the way she dressed. And she always took the clothes created for her one step further by adding something of her own, some small detail that enhanced the whole.
>
> —**HUBERT de GIVENCHY**,
> French designer and one of Audrey's close friends

Every time you feel vulnerable, every time you're scared,
every time you do what's right for you despite the naysayers,
and you don't die and the world doesn't end and you wake
up the next day, you turn vulnerability into strength. You sew
stitch by stitch; you learn ballet jèté by jèté; you get stronger
vulnerability by vulnerability. 👓

Chapter 6

THE STRENGTH
OF BEING
DELICATE

"I'll never get used to
anything. Anybody that does,
they might as well be dead."

—*Audrey*

as Holly Golightly in
Breakfast at Tiffany's

Two for the Road, 1967

t's hard to imagine what it must have been like to have Audrey's gaze on you, face to face, but it must have been something special, something magical and fierce. Because you can't love Audrey and not love her eyes. It's part of the reason her son Sean once used the word "emotional" to describe his mother to a reporter. Everything she was feeling or had ever felt seemed to live in her eyes. They were her most delicate yet noteworthy feature.

> What people seemed to like about her the most were the eyes. The eyes always got everybody. But also she had an openness and an ease about herself that people found not just lovely to look at but charming as a character trait.
>
> —BARRY PARIS,
> author of the biography *Audrey Hepburn*

Her costars played to them, and her directors played them up. Her eyes gave her acting depth and leverage. Fans couldn't help but be drawn in by them, ready to see, hear, and believe anything Audrey wanted to share. More than anything she did professionally, though, her eyes and the feelings behind them make clear that Audrey was, first and foremost, a natural nurturer, who felt just as frail as those she hoped to care for. Whether or not she really was as frail as she felt is another matter altogether, but because she felt that way, it does matter. Her nurturing instinct and her compassion for all living creatures—children, animals, even plants—remind us that her greatest longing was to mother, to be somebody's mother, and to bring a child into and up in the world on the tremendous strength of her abundant love and empathy.

> 66 She was the best that we could possibly be. She was perfectly charming and perfectly loving. She was a dream. And she was the dream that you remember when you wake up smiling. 99
>
> —RICHARD DREYFUSS,
> American actor and Audrey's costar in *Always*

The fashion photographer and designer Cecil Beaton once described Audrey's eyes as "young and sad." They did have a youthful, innocent quality to them, but sad? That's debatable. What Beaton called sad might be more keenly described as open and tender. Audrey was letting other people see her true self,

How to Steal a Million, 1966

> ❝ I was on Broadway at the same time. I used to watch her go in and out of the theater. She seemed so terribly different and sort of very angelic and sort of very ethereal. It was like some kind of fairy book person. ❞
>
> —HARRY BELAFONTE, American singer, actor, and activist recalling when both he and Audrey were starring in Broadway plays in the 1950s

66 . . . her soul was always on her face. **99**

—ROBERT WOLDERS, Audrey's significant other
and partner for the last several years of her life

and that included not only her grief and heartbreak but also her delight and gratitude, inquisitiveness and determination, intuition and compassion. She was letting her fans witness aspects of her emotional map, which is what makes us human and which helped make Audrey first a star and then a mother to us all.

> When you see *Roman Holiday*, you get the overwhelming perfume of this creature, this extraordinary, original, elegant, beautiful, gentle creature. Just radiates from the screen.
>
> —RODDY MCDOWALL, English actor and director

It wasn't just her eyes, though. Audrey had a dancer's delicacy, too, in both the way she moved and in the way she stood still. You knew she was a dancer just by the turn of her foot, the twist of her arm, and the way her head appeared to just softly rest on her neck with the lightest touch. She was an otherworldly, glorious creature to behold.

But it wasn't just her eyes and her body language that expressed her delicacy. It was also her voice. If she was a dream to watch, it was the sound of her voice that rocked you to sleep.

66 Audrey was amazing.
You could see her soul
through her eyes. And
she was gentle and calm
and deep. And very much
herself. 99

—JOAN STALEY, American actress

Funny Face, 1957

Every word was gently measured, articulated with generosity, and presented calmly and warmly as an auditory gift to whomever was on the receiving end.

> "I realize that most of us live on the skin—on the surface—without appreciating just how wonderful it is simply to be alive at all."
>
> —*Audrey*

She rarely spoke aggressively or defensively; she was ever the diplomat. The impact of her composure and sincerity cannot be overestimated. It doesn't matter how elegant you look or how elegantly you walk. If you open your mouth and hostility and insincerity come pouring out, whatever gracefulness you think you've achieved suddenly vanishes.

But Audrey's way of interacting with people wasn't effortless. You have to care about the people you're with, the situation you're in, and the kind of person you want to be. You have to listen and not overreact. You have to make the choice to reply with delicacy even when you'd rather give someone a big piece of your mind.

Love in the Afternoon, 1957

> *She made it true. What she said and what she felt, she made it so clear that her partner had to react the proper way. She drew them into reality. She understood the character and she demonstrated it to the audience in a very subtle way. You knew always what was going through her mind.*
>
> —**BILLY WILDER**, screenwriter and director

Audrey was a natural at this kind of dance. That doesn't mean it wasn't strenuous and tiring, however. Audrey once made the observation, "If I had lived in London or New York or Hollywood, it would have been outlandish. I never liked the city. I always wanted the countryside." Part of her love for the countryside may have been that it offered her a reprieve from the effort that delicacy demands. At home, in rural Switzerland, she could be delicate only for herself and her family. "Besides," she said, "there is something about society and life in the city that oppresses me, a procedure of obliteration. The air is polluted, the backfire of cars is reminiscent of guns, and the noise is so bad you can't hear properly."

Opposite: *Wait Until Dark*, 1967

"We are all grown-up children, really. Our lives are made up of adulthood and childhood, all together. So one should go back in search of what was loved and found to be real."

—Audrey

Roman Holiday, 1953

> "I do think there are things, experiences in childhood that form you for the rest of your life. . . . But a child is a child is a child, you live by the day."
>
> —*Audrey*

Even if you're an urban dweller and can't imagine living anywhere else, you might remember what Audrey valued about the countryside and try to incorporate it into your daily experience. To cultivate a sense of delicacy, immerse yourself in nature, spending time away from the harsh lights and sounds of the city and its crowds. Walk where there is a canopy of trees

> 66 Yet while developing her radiance, she has too much innate candor to take on the gloss of artificiality that Hollywood is apt to demand of its queens. Her voice is peculiarly personal . . . it has the quality of heartbreak. 99
>
> —CECIL BEATON,
> fashion photographer and designer

Love in the Afternoon, 1957

> "What I've always had, and maybe what I was born with, was an enormous love of people, children, I loved them when I was little, I used to embarrass my mother by trying to pick babies out of prams at the market."
>
> —Audrey

overhead and dirt underfoot or where there's only blue sky and sand below. Trust that enough time and space in nature will bring out your strong but delicate side.

People have long wondered how Audrey managed to take the world in such a kind, considerate stride and remain above the fray. If you asked her, she probably would have said it was thanks to the people around her—her family, her supportive costars, and her perceptive directors. That may be so. But her garden had something to do with it, too. Her long walks through the snow had something to do with it, as did the plants she tended and the dogs that followed her devotedly from room to room, from carpet to grass.

As Audrey put it, "It's the flowers you choose, the music you play, the smile you have waiting. I want [my home] to be gay and cheerful, a haven in this troubled world."

Funny Face, 1957

> "Once she sensed that she could trust somebody, she'd do anything for them. And if she were disappointed in them, it would be the end of the world for her."
>
> —ROBERT WOLDERS,
> Audrey's significant other and partner for the
> last several years of her life

It was Mother Nature who allowed Audrey to be that kind of Audrey. You know, the one who could make a prostitute seem virtuous. She taught us that being delicate and embracing your emotions isn't a weakness but is necessary for living well. A willingness to be emotional and delicate can make it possible to achieve what we hope to be: true to ourselves. Audrey was true in her performances, and she was true in her life. She taught us to replace ruthless ambition with the more nuanced and interesting delicacy of emotional truth. When we do, we are likely to discover that we can go even further than we ever intended. ●◕

Charade, 1963

THE SKILL OF BEING LUCKY

"Did I tell you how divinely
and utterly happy I am?"

—*Audrey*

as Holly Golightly in
Breakfast at Tiffany's

"I'm a good girl, I am!"

—*Audrey* as Eliza Doolittle in *My Fair Lady*

M uch of what's been written about Audrey and her life has placed great significance on the tragic: the abandonment by her father when she was barely old enough to tell time let alone comprehend the tremendous hole his disappearance would leave behind, the traumatic years of fear and hunger during World War II, and later the miscarriages and the two marriages that didn't work out.

There is little doubt that these and other difficulties impacted Audrey and her family in ways big and small throughout her life. But people have always had struggles, and there is little use in overemphasizing heartbreak; it's already ubiquitous. Far more worthwhile is to accept the reality that everyone is marred by something. It doesn't really matter what cards life dealt Audrey so much as how she chose to play.

If she had ever been asked to describe herself in a single word, it seems likely Audrey might have chosen "lucky." It's a word and an idea she came back to throughout her life, and she used it to make sense of the extraordinary life she never expected to have and the extraordinary people she met and befriended along the way.

On how she came to be cast in *Roman Holiday*, Audrey said, "I had incredible luck. But I was not an overnight story. My mother and I lived in one room in London. I had no money and worked for eight years as a total unknown, hoofing my way through dance shows, television, and bits in movies . . . I'd acted so very little. I'd had no training, no preparation. But I'd been working many, many years before that 'magical' 120 minutes happened."

---

66 There was poetry and motion in anything she touched. 99

—LOEKIE VAN OVEN, a Gaskell dancer who took
Audrey under her wing after the war

Discipline is something Audrey knew an awfully lot about, although that didn't stop her from making infuriatingly charming declarations to the press such as "I'm not one who has rules. I am not a person who must have so many hours of sleep so that my skin will look good. I love to walk, so I do get lots of air . . . lots and lots of oxygen. And I sleep marvelously well. I need eight or nine hours to make me completely happy; otherwise I long for a nap. But if I don't have one, it doesn't destroy me. I'm very relaxed and unmethodical about myself. I do what I have to do and let it go at that."

Walking! Relaxing! *Breathing.* These are Audrey's self-professed "rules" of living. Oh, if only we could follow such guidelines and know that we too would be lucky enough

Roman Holiday, 1953

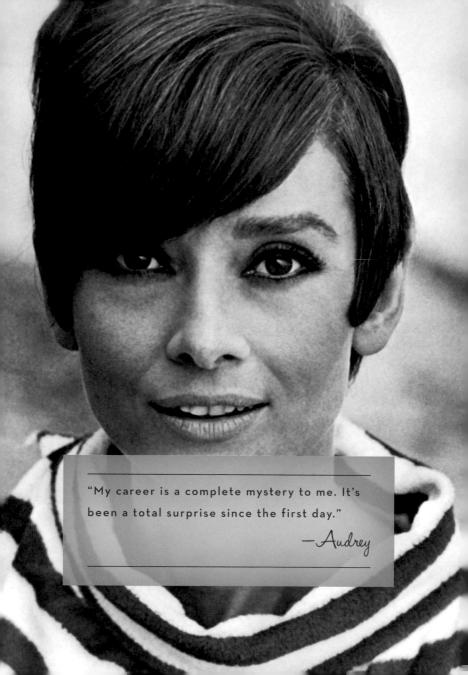

"My career is a complete mystery to me. It's been a total surprise since the first day."

—Audrey

to wake up as effortlessly elegant as Audrey, radiating her signature kindness and joy. Because that's what it is really about, isn't it? It's not the sunglasses or the dress or the haircut or the success. It's her smile. It's her attention, the way she looks at her costar or her interviewer, and you know she's really listening. According to a *Cosmopolitan* magazine profile: "In talking about herself—or any subject from artichokes to zebras—she takes up one point at a time, never skips or flashes back. When she reads, she reads; when she fits, she fits; when she talks clothes, she talks clothes; when she sits under a drier, she simply sits and dries. 'She is the only actress I've ever had who doesn't gab, read, knit, wriggle, pick her teeth, eat a lettuce and tomato sandwich,' says her hairdresser."

Movies and fairytales may suggest otherwise, but, here in reality, luck never just drops out of the clear, blue sky. It comes from every single thing we do as well as every single thing we don't do. Audrey knew that. She invoked the role luck played in her life over and over again, but she also knew the right conditions in which luck thrives: during moments of humility, dedication, and hard work. After all, you can't get lucky if you've given up. If you want to be there when luck shows up, you better be disciplined.

It doesn't matter that Holly Golightly tried to convince herself otherwise; people do belong to other people, if you work hard and you are lucky enough, that is. So it is that at the end of *Breakfast at Tiffany's*, Holly and Cat discover they belong to each other and to Paul Varjak or "Fred" or whatever Holly feels like calling him. And in *Roman Holiday*, Princess Ann, when her holiday is over, finds that she does not belong to Joe Bradley, much as we and she and he want her to. She belongs to the world. Audrey herself, however, represented something a little different. She worked hard and cultivated luck so that *we* could belong to *her*. Not that we had anything to do with it. She chose us. See, we're already lucky. Who wouldn't want Audrey?

Some time after Audrey died, Blake Edwards, who directed *Breakfast at Tiffany's*, said, "I think there are a few people in one's life that you never really feel that they're gone. I have to remind myself that [Audrey] isn't around."

There's a good reason it doesn't feel like Audrey's really gone. She isn't. She is still here. And not just in her movies as her good friend Connie Wald suggested. Not even just in her exemplary work for UNICEF at the end of her life. She's part of the people who love her. Audrey once told an interviewer, "Living is like tearing through a museum. Not until later do you really start absorbing what you saw, thinking about it, looking it up in a book and remembering—because you can't take it all in at once." It's difficult to take Audrey all in at once,

"I had never seen anyone more disciplined, more gracious, or more dedicated to her work than Audrey. There was no ego."

—FRED ZINNEMANN,
who directed Audrey in the movie *The Nun's Story*

"If my world were to cave in tomorrow, I would look back on all the pleasures, excitements, and worthwhilenesses I have been lucky enough to have had. Not the sadnesses, not my miscarriages, or my father leaving home, but the joy of everything else. It will have been enough."

—*Audrey*

and perhaps that's why she feels very much alive in our hearts and minds.

At the end of *Roman Holiday* our princess says, "I don't know how to say goodbye. I can't think of any words." And Gregory Peck as Joe Bradley replies, "Don't try."

And so we won't. We'll just try to keep living like Audrey, making good use of all the wonderful things she had to teach us.

Opposite: *Breakfast at Tiffany's*, 1961

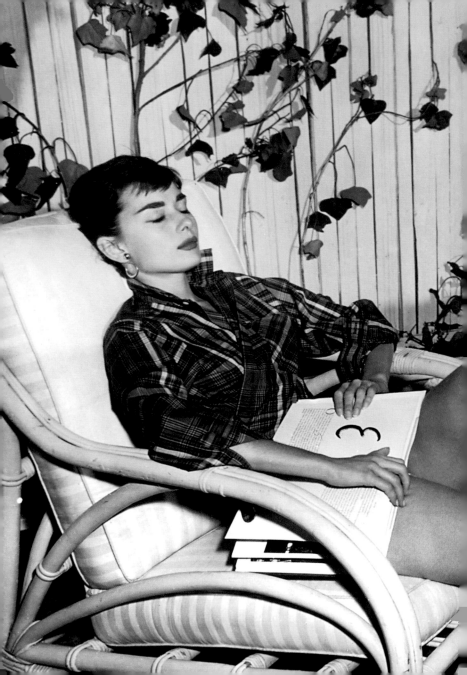

AFTERWORD

"I decided years ago to take life unconditionally, and I never expected it to do anything special for me. Yet I've accomplished far more than I ever hoped to, and most of the time it happened without my ever seeking it."

—*Audrey*

to Rex Reed on the set of *Bloodline*

started this book thinking about what other people thought. Quite literally the book opens with a description of other people's reactions to Audrey, where she was from, who she was. So it seems only fitting to come out the other side and end the book thinking about what I think. You'll have your own thoughts when you finish reading the book and arrive here, but what do I think having finished writing it?

I think that of all the strong, charming, and enchanting characters she portrayed onscreen, Audrey Hepburn was, off screen, more like one than all the others: Susy Hendrix. Now, unless you're president of the Audrey Hepburn fan club, you may be asking yourself, who's Susy and why am I only hearing about her now? Susy is the character Audrey played in one of her slightly later movies, which, sadly, hasn't gotten much play in these pages.

Wait Until Dark came out in 1967, and Audrey received her fifth (and last) Academy Award nomination for Best Actress for her portrayal of Susy. She didn't win, though. Not because she wasn't great in the role (she was) but because guess who the other nominees were? Anne Bancroft for *The Graduate*, Faye Dunaway for *Bonnie and Clyde*, Katharine Hepburn for *Guess Who's Coming to Dinner*, and Edith Evans for *The Whisperers*. (If you don't know Edith Evans, she was a tremendously well-regarded English actress, and *The Whisperers* has got to be one of the darkest, most depressing films about aging and community responsibility and social safety nets ever to come out of Britain, which is saying something.) Needless to say, the competition was fierce, and Katharine won. It seems somehow especially poignant that the last time Audrey was nominated

Two for the Road, 1967

"I was given an outlook on life by my mother . . .
It was frowned upon not to think of others first.
It was frowned upon not to be disciplined . . .
During the last winter of the war, we had no food
whatsoever, and my aunt said to me, 'Tomorrow
we'll have nothing to eat, so the best thing to
do is stay in bed and conserve our energy.'
That very night, a member of the underground
brought us food—flour, jam, oatmeal, cans of
butter . . . When I hit rock-bottom, there [was]
always something there for me."

—Audrey

for an Academy Award for Best Actress she lost to the other Hepburn, the one Hubert de Givenchy had assumed he was meeting some fourteen years earlier when Audrey's star was only just beginning to rise.

Bonnie and Clyde, *The Graduate*, and *Guess Who's Coming to Dinner* were all also nominated for Best Picture, Best Director, Best Actor, and Best Supporting Actress that year. There are reasons *Wait Until Dark* was not, but that isn't to say

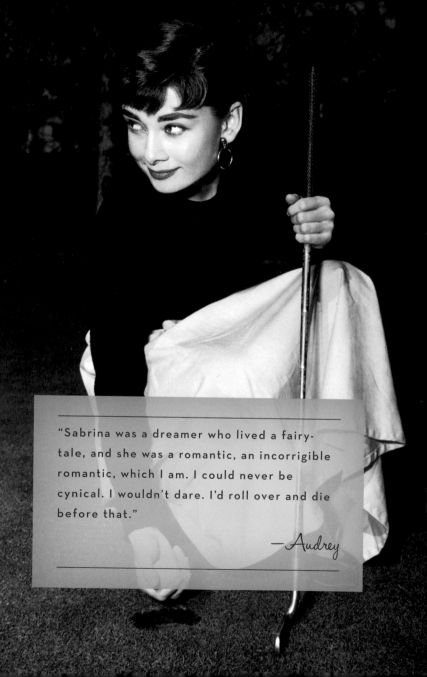

"Sabrina was a dreamer who lived a fairy-tale, and she was a romantic, an incorrigible romantic, which I am. I could never be cynical. I wouldn't dare. I'd roll over and die before that."

—*Audrey*

it isn't good. It's wonderful. It's just a smaller movie than the others, and Audrey is the biggest thing about it. Even before filming had begun, Audrey had known she was ready to leave Hollywood. *Wait Until Dark* wasn't her last film, but it would be nearly a decade before she made another, and not one of the final four films she would make later offers a part anywhere near the richness of a Sabrina or a Susy. Mel Ferrer, Audrey's husband at the time of filming and also the producer of *Wait Until Dark*, once said that Audrey had known as soon as she finished reading the script that she wanted to play Susy, that, usually, she took a few days to decide whether or not she was interested in a part but that Susy had spoken to her instantly.

Susy Hendrix is a newly blind newlywed (married to a photographer), who over the course of the film is terrorized by a violent criminal played by a practically unrecognizable Alan Arkin (well, unrecognizable assuming you know him more for *Little Miss Sunshine* and less for *Catch-22*). At first glance, the story appears to be that of just another waif miraculously overcoming the cruelties of humanity in a plot that doesn't totally add up, which is what most of the white, male critics of the day saw and reviewed. But what I saw and what I suspect Audrey saw, what made her want to take on the role, is the story of a woman, blind only in the physical sense, and her very

Opposite: *Sabrina*, 1954

Paris When It Sizzles, 1964

> "I'm like Cat here, a no-name slob. We belong to nobody, and nobody belongs to us. We don't even belong to each other."
>
> —*Audrey*
>
> as Holly Golightly in *Breakfast at Tiffany's*

young upstairs neighbor, a girl, puberty infuriatingly just out of reach, who together use their unassuming powers of grace, style, humor, strength, gentility, and luck to outwit three men, who can see but only in the physical sense.

There are other women Audrey played who shared many of these same qualities, but there's a particular naturalness to her Susy that is unlike anything else she did in front of the camera. Maybe it's the simplicity of the world in which we meet Susy at the start of the movie. Maybe it feels especially natural and simple to me because the entire movie was filmed on St. Luke's Place in New York City's Greenwich Village, three blocks from my own apartment and just a couple of doors down from the branch of the public library where I wrote much of this book. It helps, too, that Susy and her husband live in a modest one-bedroom

Opposite: *War and Peace*, 1956

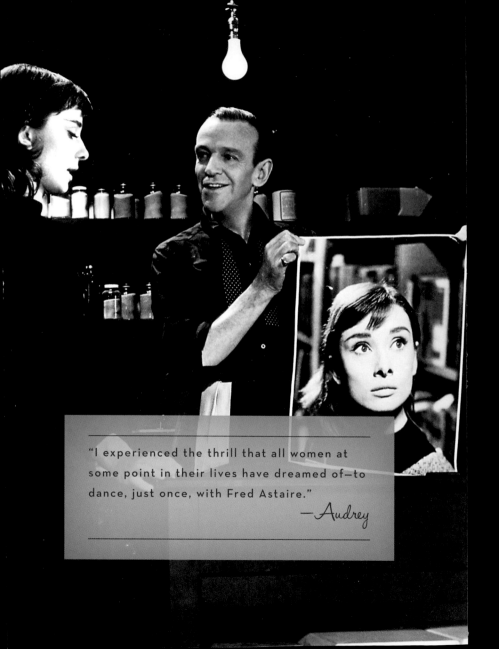

"I experienced the thrill that all women at some point in their lives have dreamed of—to dance, just once, with Fred Astaire."

—Audrey

basement apartment, which, naturally and not coincidentally, gets horrible light. He's a freelance photographer, and she's recently gone back to school and wears chic fitted turtleneck sweaters and short skirts. In other words, they're just like us.

> She saw it as pure luck. She could not understand why people wanted her to be in films and what they thought was so special about her. So she made up for it by working extra hard.
>
> **SEAN FERRER**, Audrey's firstborn son

We want our stars to be relatable, but Audrey is the rare celebrity who not only was, but managed to express it without losing any of her effervescence. It's difficult to imagine feeling quite as strongly about Audrey as we do if we'd never seen how vulnerable and insecure she could be and how much that made her care. She wasn't impervious to other people's opinions; none of us are, but Audrey showed us that was okay. All living like Audrey really means is to try and keep trying and never stop. Luckily, that's something every single one of us is capable of. You don't even have to wait until dark. You can start right now. ●◗

Opposite: *Funny Face*, 1957

"Do I detect a look of disapproval in your eye? Tough beans buddy, 'cause that's the way it's gonna be."

—*Audrey*

as Holly Golightly in
Breakfast at Tiffany's

Breakfast at Tiffany's, 1961

A
MOVIE
ABOUT THOSE
WHO APPRECIATE THE
FINEST
THINGS IN
LIFE...
FOR
FREE!

audrey
HEPBURN
AND
PETER
O'TOOLE
GIVE
A LESSON IN
LOVE AND
LARCENY IN
WILLIAM
WYLER'S

HOW
TO
STEAL
a
million

20.
CENTURY-FOX

ELI WALLACH
HUGH GRIFFITH
CHARLES BOYER

A WILLIAM WYLER-FRED KOHLMAR PRODUCTION   Produced by FRED KOHLMAR   Directed by WILLIAM WYLER
Screenplay by HARRY KURNITZ   PANAVISION   COLOR by DE LUXE

Acknowledgments

I find the word "acknowledgment" to be a bit long on letters and to come up a bit short on meaning. Acknowledging one another is the very least we can do. I prefer the word gratitude. We can thank Latin's *gratus* and the root *grat* for not only gratitude but its many sisters, including: grateful, ingratiate, congratulate. Even grace can be traced back to the same beginning. So, in the name of Audrey, my gratitude to those who have made this book possible:

Holly Rubino and Evan Helmlinger for shepherding this project from idea to reality and graciously inviting me to be a part of their vision,

And Jessica Regel for her uncanny ability to generate side hustles and to whom I owe so much of the fun I've had and the work I've done,

And the Hudson Park branch of the New York Public Library for its characters both on and off the page,

And Casey Scieszka for being one of the friendliest badasses I know,

And Liz Ichniowski for having her wedding on the Aeolian Island of Salina, because she knew I had never been to Italy,

And Alex Levenson and Lynda Reddy for their poker faces but also their real faces,

And Katie Klumper and Joanna Myssura for all the texts but especially the ones with the photos I will never be able to unsee,

And all three of the Downs-Anderson sisters (Sarah, Abby, and Monika) for being my favorite uppers outside of coffee,

And Jill Brenner for her friendship, because she is exactly the kind of friend I hoped I would have when I grew up,

And Melissa Opper for her friendship, too, because she is exactly the kind of friend I needed when I was young and who I am honored has stuck around,

And Ruby Bolaria for refusing to let her considerable intelligence make her cynical,

And Jennie Baird for seeing in people and in situations things I would never notice,

And Amy DiTullio for being the best thing about America Online and who may call me Vic for as long as she likes, which I hope is forever,

And Roshni Naik for saving me even though she probably doesn't know that she did,

And Daisy Freund and Mary Dain and Megan McGowan for their taste in wine, poems, women, and tiny hats—you are each unstoppable,

And Carmen Ribera for always finding an excuse to use her outdoor voice indoors,

And Marcia Rooney for her commitment to celebration and for Napa, all of Napa,

And Jeannie Ponn for her ability to envision something and make it happen and for never giving up,

And Mary Kay Paonessa for accepting Everyone,

And Suzie Loustalot for listening to my very first word and every word thereafter,

And Michael Twigg for giving the most disarming reality checks and for being the Unsinkable Michael Twigg,

And Camden Pell and Baby Diva Pell, who are still en route to their parents but will both have arrived by the time this book is also born, for being the little tiny beacons of hope only babies can be and for being absolutely perfect now and always. Welcome.

MOVIES

Always. Directed by Steven Spielberg. 1989. Universal City, CA: Universal Pictures.

Bloodline. Directed by Terence Young. 1979. Hollywood, CA: Paramount Pictures.

Breakfast at Tiffany's. Directed by Blake Edwards. 1961. Hollywood, CA: Paramount Pictures.

Charade. Directed by Stanley Donen. 1963. Universal City, CA: Universal Pictures.

The Children's Hour. Directed by William Wyler. 1961. Beverly Hills, CA: United Artists.

Funny Face. Directed by Stanley Donen. 1957. Hollywood, CA: Paramount Pictures.

Green Mansions. Directed by Mel Ferrer. 1959. Beverly Hills, CA: Metro-Goldwyn-Mayer Studios.

How to Steal a Million. Directed by William Wyler. 1966. Los Angeles, CA: 20th Century Fox.

Love in the Afternoon. Directed by Billy Wilder. 1957. Los Angeles, CA: Allied Artists.

My Fair Lady. Directed by George Cukor. 1964. Burbank, CA: Warner Bros.

The Nun's Story. Directed by Fred Zinnemann. 1959. Burbank, CA: Warner Bros.

Paris When It Sizzles. Directed by Richard Quine. 1964. Hollywood, CA: Paramount Pictures.

Robin and Marian. Directed by Richard Lester. 1976. Culver City, CA: Columbia Pictures.

Roman Holiday. Directed by William Wyler. 1953. Hollywood, CA: Paramount Pictures.

Sabrina. Directed by Billy Wilder. 1954. Hollywood, CA: Paramount Pictures.

Two for the Road. Directed by Stanley Donen. 1967. Los Angeles, CA: 20th Century Fox.

The Unforgiven. Directed by John Huston. 1960. Beverly Hills, CA: United Artists.

Wait Until Dark. Directed by Terence Young. 1967. Burbank, CA: Warner Bros.

War and Peace. Directed by King Vidor. 1956. Hollywood, CA: Paramount Pictures.

Photo Credits

Photos courtesy of Photofest:

Pages ii, vi–vii, viii, 13, 14, 21, 22, 30, 35, 36, 41, 50, 69, 80, 104, 107, 114, 121, 128, 132, 134–135, 136, 150–151, 152, 158, 161, 164–165, 176, 187

Photos courtesy of Paramount Pictures/Photofest:

Pages 2, 5, 8, 27, 28–29 (Photographer: Bill Avery), 32–33, 38–39, 44–45, 47, 54, 57, 58–59, 76, 86–87, 89, 94, 101, 113, 116–117, 125, 142, 147 (Photographer: Bill Avery), 155, 156–157, 162, 170, 172–173, 175, 178–179

Photos courtesy of 20th Century Fox/Photofest:

Pages 42 (Photographer: Vincent Rossell), 66–67, 78–79, 84, 90 (Photographer: Vincent Rossell), 93, 96–97, 99, 126–127, 131, 166, 168, 180

Photos courtesy of Universal Pictures/Photofest:

Pages xvi–1, 16–17, 48–49, 60, 64, 70, 72–73, 102–103, 110–111, 118, 149

Photos courtesy of Allied Artists Int'l/Photofest:

Pages 24–25, 138–139, 144–145

Photos courtesy of Warner Bros./Photofest:

Pages 6–7, 10–11, 52–53, 75, 83, 108, 122–123

Photo courtesy of Warner Bros./Seven Arts/Photofest:

Page 141

Photo courtesy of United Artists/Photofest:

Page 19

Photo courtesy of MGM/Photofest:

Pages 62–63

Photo courtesy of Michael Twigg:

Page 190

About the Author

VICTORIA LOUSTALOT was born in California and lives in New York. She earned her BA as well as her MFA from Columbia University. *Living Like Audrey* is her second book of nonfiction. Her first is the memoir *This Is How You Say Goodbye*.